HOLDING DIS

GW00870764

Holding Distance

GRACE WILENTZ

Green Bottle Press

First published in 2019
by Green Bottle Press
83 Grove Avenue
London N10 2AL
www.greenbottlepress.com

Cover design by Økvik Design
Cover image © Les Cunliffe/Dreamstime.com
Typeset by CB editions, London
Printed in England by Imprint Digital, Exeter EX5 5HY

ISBN 978-1-910804-15-5

Contents

Cat's Cradle

With a loop of string
hands make figures.
Each variation's simple geometry
tracing its way back to the Cat's Cradle –
an even number of taut lines
hinting at a basket,
a shallow trough.

These string figures pass to waiting hands,
fingers splayed as a rack
ready to open into the next form.
All shapes are possible with practice:
Diamonds, Candles
(in parallel for ceremony),
the Manger.

We never ask where the names come from,
but we keep them.
The game is old,
played from pole to pole
and from point to invisible point
on the equatorial band.

Girls learn it,
play it, teach it,
memorise the names,
know what figures may follow in series:

the Cat's Eye and the Soldier's Bed
(a simple cot),
Fish in a Dish,
Jacob's Ladder.

Two Crowns is a dead end.
So is the Clock.

The game trains the hands to hold distance,
movement with elegance,
and for the mind:
that transformation is possible,
and may be swift.

The Deal

A bubble rose
in Vesuvius
out of nothing.

From one, bubbles
multiplied in
number, pressures too.

And so people turned
into sculptures seared
and sealed in ash.

At seven,
or at any age,
I can't know

their fear,
but I know
my own.

Children are always
at the mercy
of the deal.

My mother rubs
her yellow calluses
smooth with pumice

from the site.
The lightness of
that little rock,

its pores fascinate
for hours
in the tub.

My fingertips
in wrinkles
turn it over.

Solid Gold Bathtub

I grew up sure I'd seen the ghost
of Texas Guinan
in the doorframe of my bedroom one night.

She lived here, owned this building
from basement to rooftop
before it was divided up
into a shop floor, a boiler room
and a rectangle of walled garden.

Texas lit out of Waco,
and became herself:
lawless, fearless, savvy with a dollar,

the first movie cowgirl,
'Queen of the West',
emcee of her 300 Club up on 54th
where she greeted all the rich boys
with her signature:
'Hello, sucker!'

She hid the booze,
in case of a raid,
glimmering bronze and copper,
in the triangle of light cast
by the hideaway door that opened
just enough to slip though.

No stranger to roundups,
the walk to a waiting black maria,
a breeze through the Jefferson Market Jail,
before the short journey home

to 17 West 8th, full of her antiques
and her gewgaws.

Rumour had it she bought herself
a solid gold bathtub.
My father said it vanished
when she died.

Or was it stashed too?
Hidden first
and then forgotten –
solid and shimmering
under a film of dust.

I scraped at every crack
(there were many)
and dropped pennies
through gaps
in the floorboards,
listening
for the sound
of metal bouncing
off metal,
unsure
if I believed in her ghost
or believed in the stories.

Hand, Writing

It took all my focus and patience
to learn to write in script.
Hours of practice, rising early to sit
alone in the classroom tracing a letter
again and again. Knowing the room's
four walls and the silence, and
understanding that I had to catch up –
in private school you do not print.

It was this routine of rising early
to practice alone, through which I felt
each letter's form slope into meaning.
I continued this task of tracing the letter,
below the blackboard with
yesterday's lesson swept into swirls
by a wet sponge. The hand writing,
the letter repeating, across the page.

Summer Accomplishments, After Death

I cleaned the empty apartment,
painted the walls White Linen,
sanded the floor on my knees for a week,
patched everything up with plaster and caulk.

I wrote my husband's footstone,
and worked in my studio, portrait sculpture mostly.
I rented (on my own) the empty apartment,
and unstuck all those windows, carelessly painted shut.

I painted the front gate black for the summer,
emptied the boiler's full tank of water.
I replaced the bolts – *all* the bolts?
I changed my name.

I was left with all this love
and nothing to do with it.

The Lioness

No swimming this summer. The lake is closed.
When the circus came through
elephants contaminated the water.

We are older anyway,
sitting in the dark bedroom
passing a paperback found in the move.

Was it a book of women's fantasies or of men's?
There was the swim-team threesome
at the edge of the pool, where the lane lines

were strings of plastic discs, buoyed up
and stretching out across the aqua blue water.
Chlorine in the nostrils and the

slap of feet on wet tile.
The team uniform, electric blue,
and the way each body wore it.

In the last chapter: the lioness,
the woman who lowered herself
into an animal, and the man

who feared her, but drew near to her
through the long grasses
one hand raised to ask for her protection,

while her tail swept to show herself,
and to hide herself
so as never to be quite seen.

She lands a paw
and the dust rises,
though she is still when he

9

moves to shimmy under her,
clings to her belly and
lifts his knees to grip her flanks,

entering, then moving inside her.
She has to crouch to lay him down after.
Her spine, curling and uncurling

as she slowly departs him,
is the most common waveform,
the mountain system, an arc, S.

Cancer Diary II

When you pay attention
to what you're doing
it can become interesting.
Are you looking?

Manage lymph damage.
Stimulate drainage from
affected arm to unaffected.
Press behind clavicles
along sternum, shoulder, arm.

The interrelation of the system
is its self-destructive capability, inbuilt.

No way to make cells aware
they are abnormal.
A gene is wired to maybe
grind a cell into soup.
DNA directs RNA.

Reception and then reaction.
The cell is not
a body or a breast.

Lots of hand-outs.
Support groups.
Smith Farm, Virginia.
Green tea, clover, soy.

Things that annoy you –
nakedness,
the vein of your left arm,
tapped out.

Coral Castle

Demented Ed built it,
still no one knows how.
The neighbours mostly ignored him,
his wizened little silhouette
working against the Florida sun.

One local looking back recalls
the small box Ed set up on a tripod,
the pinhole he cut in it
and the cloth he draped to cover himself.

This array of coral slabs,
arranged into henges and dolmens,
is carved to a cold home,
that is also a tribute, and a gutted abbey
open to the air under a ceiling of sky.

The Florida Table is an homage
to the state's weird geography.
Then there is the Sun Couch, the Well
and the Feast of Love Table
carved in the shape of a heart.

The Repentance Corner adjoins the barbeque.
The Throne Room, majestic,
is where his love could climb up,
take her pick of elevated seats
topped by carvings of the moon and Saturn.

The recollection is that he worked secretly,
always at night, never showing his methods,
alone, removing and moving
lumps of honeycomb coral from the sea,

heavier in weight than the blocks
composing the pyramids,
his technology unknowable,
to go down with him when he died, loveless.

The Coral Castle didn't win her as he thought it would.
Realising this, how different it would have looked
as he walked it empty and alone,
trailing his hands against the rough braille of its walls.

Still, he knew the lightness that is possible,
as when a pockmarked slab of coral,
that once gave some shelter in a changing ocean,
hefts its own tonne weight,
scrapes itself loose,
floats effortless as the ouija's planchette,
and hovers impossibly up from beneath the waves,
beginning its crossing to stand upon the shore.

The Mosè

My mother and I arrive to San Pietro in Vincoli.
The Mosè rests behind its double doors,
heavy against weather and time.

One nun consults another,
and together they wrap me,
waist to ankle in a large bright sheet.

It is early.
Two coins clatter in an empty tin
and we can go inside.

The month is August.
What is this chill?
Our steps send an echo.
A creased map in the hand
becomes flutter in the rafters.

The Mosè is at the back,
frozen in hesitation, ready to rise.
He is all sinew, unlike the starving arm of Christ
limp in pietà after pietà.

His body is marble strength,
the sheer force applied
to fashion stone into a man.
It is written that he lisped and wished
to grow away from God's command
that is unfolding still,
envelops us here.
Pigeons in the square suddenly disperse.

We stand before the Mosè,
our arrival like every other in this church

catching him off guard.
He has been waiting for us to come clear from the shadows,
hesitant, unsure if he should rise.

Belly of the Whale

After days
of not speaking to anyone
the sound of my voice
echoes back to me,
like the voice of a stranger.

Ribs come together above me
as church rafters.

Time is parcelled out in the silences between
the slow-beating life of this beast,
the groan of its body,
the shrill song of its calls.

I remember watching it rise,
mountainous.
I considered its swooping frown and thought:
how very like a clown's mouth!
before the lips opened with a yawn
and the suck of water pulled me in like a riptide.

And then: silence, unlit dark.

Brief, but there are the moments when
I feel myself to be
in a darkened theatre.

Sometimes, I can feel us diving,
weightless, as I dream.

The Irish Hunger Memorial, Battery Park

for Rod Keating and Caroline Stone

On the day I'm leaving home, we discover it,
entering through the tunnel
of fluorescent backlit clips and scraps of a story,
too long to tell coherently.

Layered over the eerie glow
are poems, parliamentary reports,
letters, recipes, names, statistics, songs,
and blank spaces, still to be engraved.

When we come through it into the day
before us is a tilted half acre on Battery Park.
It must have been started
before the skyline was transformed.

We follow the path, passing
the cottage from Attymass, County Mayo,
that is no replica, was once someone's home,
until we're peering out beyond the island's southern tip,

over the Hudson with its ghost pier disintegrating,
the Statue of Liberty, Ellis Island.
Looking out in stillness, I wonder if we're seen
by the work-a-days in the offices above.

I'm carrying a book on the essay, his gift to me,
and the scarf with sparkling threads
that she took off and handed me
through the car window.

The old cycle of consciousness versus craving
is broken, momentarily, when I realise

I was in need of people to say goodbye to.
Brought back to the present

by the surprise of this memorial
to the devastation of hunger.
The river before us, like a clearing,
mimicking time moving us forward.

The Iguana Dreams of Her Mom

Lazy I slept through the lunar eclipse and dreamt of my mother.
She has visited me only twice – in some Midwestern supermarket,
and again, in the stall of a Bangkok street merchant. Each time
the feeling was fuller than a phantom limb, for I think I have my
heart back. Before the backward fall of waking, where the strings
of grief catch me and make me move. I have lived through two
eclipses – saw one on a beach with my mother, missed one in a
dream with her too.

Castlewellan Carwash

I have always wanted this –
sponge forming suds,
bits like lace, flying.

Shielded from the soapy ropes,
and the scouring blasts clouding
the laminated glass,

water runs in streams,
too thick to be seen through.
While we are warm and dry

and together here
for the long drive home,
and for now, the spectacle.

Halter

For two years Dorothy kept everyone out: visitors, even me.
If a hand fell on the bedroom doorknob, she'd tense in another room:
Don't go in there, you'll mess up my papers.

By the time we discovered what she knew
(the roof had fallen in during the last record storm)
pale blue insulation covered everything in drifts.

She made up her mind to go, the mind that was already hollowing out,
little sinkholes out of nowhere pulling its calm surface
down to chaos, and then nothing.

That August, with the election looming and the Virginia heat,
she rested and worried while we carted away twenty-two sacks full.
Backwards and forwards in what we started calling the Havisham room

insulation disintegrated in our hands as we grasped for more,
until the room was like before, except for the exposed chipboard above
and the smell of all the seasons that had blown through it.

We searched to salvage, fingered her colourful silks, still folded
though water-stained and ruined by mould,
we untangled costume jewellery (she bought herself a piece with every pay cheque).

Opening the drawer that held her lingerie sets protectively wrapped in brittle tissue,
beside a copy of the *Kama Sutra*, her helpful friends from church hurried out,
and I was left to empty the drawer alone.

At sixty-five, Dorothy, my grandmother, retired and by then twice divorced,
cut and sewed herself a yellow calico halter top modelled on a Vogue pattern.
No sleeves, but a strap around the neck. She'd slip it on to haul out

her portable Remington to type the Reverend's notes, details of Sunday's service,
requests for auction donations, and updates from the book group and the
Pie-of-the-Month club. One of her church friends told me how Dorothy once

wore the halter to deliver the newsletter. How the Reverend looked her up and down
before beginning his rounds to each desk in the church office
stopping to ask if Dorothy would ever learn to dress her age.

He stared at the scalloped folds of her underarm
before scanning the newsletter for typos
and sending her back to type it again.

I hold the book in the room we've come so close to restoring,
and try to imagine her at the bookstore
buying the *Kama Sutra*.

Did she wear the yellow calico halter?
Walking to the counter, did she look the cashier in the eye?
I think maybe she did, look at him and smile.

Covers

On the box of magazines in the basement
beside the unopened bread-maker,
I find this handwritten note:
Moved from living room settee, September 1998.
On each magazine cover, women set their limbs in poses.

I lift magazines by the armful,
place them in a clear blue recycling bag
and make a private wish
that my life might amount to more
than being a good companion to a man.

In the mix are two *New Yorkers*.
On the cover dated March 3, 1973,
a young woman reads
at the light of a green lamp
beside tall shelves of books.

While across the cover from December 19, 1942,
a woman cycles through the snow,
an evergreen tree balanced
on the handlebars of her bicycle,
her dachshund keeping pace beside her.

I too, have been content to lose myself
in the present chapter,
to rhythmically pedal the bike.
I know the cold that stings the lungs,
and have breathed through it.

What if everything I ever wanted
is what I have already received?

The Flood

Such sea legs, Noah
has to keep his eyes open in the shower
for fear of breaking his nose
on the tile walls.

He dries himself the proper way,
the way his father taught him
and wonders is it possible that he can be here,
naked in another's home.

Whose bed is this
that does not slide across the floor?
Whose windows not streaked with rain
rise above a green lawn?

Nothing creaks.
When a robin settles in the tree outside
he leans to hear if its wings whisper:
Land, at last land.

He wonders:
Why can I not breathe in the smell of salt?
Whose children are these whose feet
pad on solid ground?

He wonders:
Am I the only one who remembers?
Did I survive
the sky's complete letting go?

Can home have washed me
to another shore?
Can one step, just like that
from the heaving, pitching ark?

An Gleann Mór

You take my hand beside the waterfall
at the end of the Devil's Glen,
say, *Let's sit here a little longer.*

We should go, I say and nod
to the sun just slipped below the timberline.

Here, eat this, you say,
I want to taste plum on your lips.

Back where we began, a local man,
his finger through a ring of keys
is pulling the long steel barrier behind.

Luthier in the Forest

for David Lynch

To make a fine instrument
what's needed
is a good timber,
come from a tree
that struggled to grow.

Exposed to extremes –
the winter freeze that stunts –
forcing each ring in a little tighter,

until one day a greater solidity forms,
to hold and carry
vibration, tone, brilliance.

Eau de Campagne

She greets me like she knows me,

though I have entered this Berlin shopping centre
for the first time, and just to escape the rain.
Offering a silver sachet of perfumed oil, she says:
The secret is to put a pin in it, that way it will last the week.

I twist lipsticks, browse backlit glass bottles.
I have one just for you, she says, and nods to my backpack.
I place it on the ground and am suddenly aware
of its wear, my shabby sneakers and wet mac.

She lifts a bottle from the shelf and sprays the air,
catching its mist with her hands cupped as a tent,
fingertip touching fingertip, as she gestures
for me to come closer, quickly, before it fades.

In her bare hands is the scent of spring at its first,
before it deepens into the whole round year:
fresh-cut grass, breaking citrus peel, ripe currant,
oak moss, wood smoke, the forest after rain.

NOTES TO THE POEMS

Texas Guinan became the United States' first movie cowgirl, nicknamed 'The Queen of the West'. She purchased a home at 17 West 8th Street in New York City. When Prohibition was introduced in 1920, she became one of the first female emcees, opening a speakeasy called the 300 Club at 151 West 54th Street.

Footstones are the markers at the foot of a grave. They are generally used as an individual grave marker in conjunction with a family headstone.

Coral Castle is an oolite limestone structure created by the Latvian-American eccentric Edward Leedskalnin, located in Leisure City, Florida, in Miami-Dade County at the intersection of South Dixie Highway and Southwest 157th Avenue. The structure comprises numerous megalithic stones (mostly limestone formed from coral), each weighing several tonnes.

The *Mosè* is a sculpture by Michelangelo Buonarroti, housed in the church of San Pietro in Vincoli in Rome.

A *luthier* is someone who builds or repairs string instruments.

ACKNOWLEDGEMENTS

Acknowledgements are due to the following publications in which versions of these poems first appeared: *Poetry Ireland Review, Cyphers, Magma, The Harvard Advocate* and the Hennessy New Irish Writing series in *The Irish Times.*

My friends have been generous with their encouragement for many years. I am especially grateful to those who shared their thoughts on drafts of this manuscript: Peter Fallon, Niall McGuinness, Peig McManus, Julie Morrissy, Alexander Rothman and Rosamund Taylor.

Thank you to my teachers: Siobhán Campbell, Jorie Graham, Seamus Heaney, Paula Meehan, Paul Perry and Peter Richards for showing me the way. Heartfelt thanks to Shane McCrae for sharing his reflection on the book for the back cover.

After many years in Ireland, I've found meaningful community through writers' groups and collaborations with Kevin Conroy, Bernie Crawford, Fiona Fahey, Pauline Flynn, Jackie Gorman, Anne Leahy, Phil Lynch, Éilís Murphy and Michael Ryan.

Most of all, I am grateful to have had the opportunity to work with Jennifer Grigg, editor and publisher at the Green Bottle Press, who embraced these poems and supported me through revision and editing. For careful attention to the final form, I would like to thank Astrid Griffiths at Økvik Design, Charles Boyle at CB Editions and Marsha Swan of Iota Books.